ANTOINE'S TALE

An Extraordinary Shelter Dog's Journey

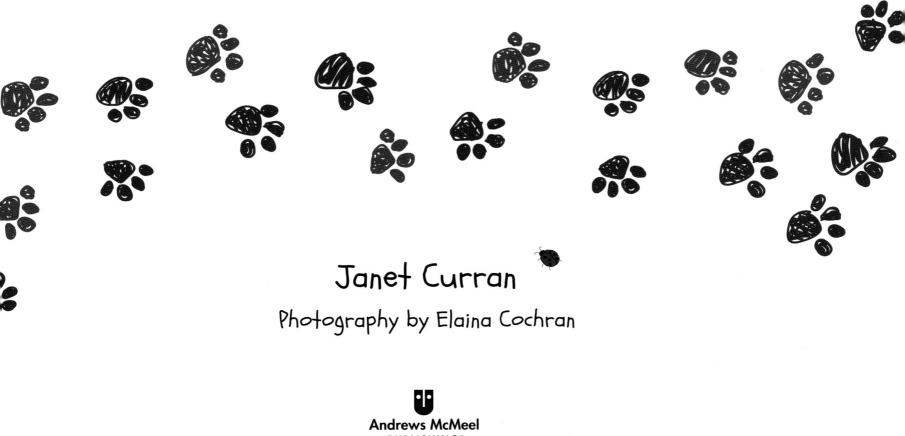

Janet Curran

Photography by Elaina Cochran

Andrews McMeel
PUBLISHING®

Antoine's Tale

Andrews McMeel Publishing
a division of Andrews McMeel Universal
1130 Walnut Street, Kansas City, Missouri 64106

www.andrewsmcmeel.com

22 23 24 25 26 TEN 10 9 8 7 6 5 4 3 2 1

ISBN: 978-1-5248-7160-4

Library of Congress Control Number: 2021945000

Made by:
1010 Printing International Ltd.
1010 Ave Xia Nan Industrial District, Yuan Zhou Town
Bo Luo County, Hui Zhou, Guangdong Province, China 516123
1st Printing—4/25/22

Photos by Janet Curran or Connie Fredman: pages 1, 2, 3, 4, 5, 6, 7, 8, 9, 10, 16, 18, 19, 20, 21, 22, 23, 25

Attention: Schools and Businesses

Andrews McMeel books are available at quantity discounts with bulk purchase
for educational, business, or sales promotional use. For information, please e-mail the
Andrews McMeel Publishing Special Sales Department: specialsales@amuniversal.com.

HI! I'm Antoine.

My name wasn't always Antoine, but we'll get to that later.
I know I just met you, but I'm excited to tell you my story.

When I was little, I spent time in two shelters and a very loving foster home. I needed a lot of care because my legs didn't work like other dogs' legs.

Then I met someone who would change my life forever. She believed I could get better and arranged for me to go to a very special hospital. I would meet with some very special doctors.

When I got there, the doctors told me I was born with
a serious infection.
Luckily, Dr. Felix had a new surgery in mind.

Dr. Super Man Felix

Although the surgery would only take a few hours,
recovery would be much longer.

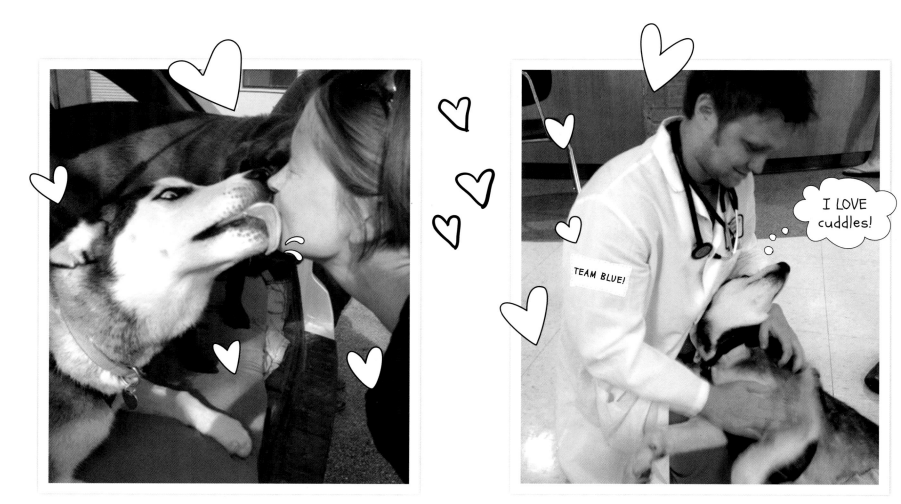

 Thanks to my new friends and doctors,
I knew I could do it!
I wanted to work hard to get better.

I only had one request before surgery. I wanted to change my name from Blue. This was the name one of the shelters had given me because of the color of my eyes. I wanted a new name that fit me better because I was feeling stronger, more powerful, and courageous. I FELT LIKE A SUPERHERO!

I wanted my name to be

ANTOINE THE GREAT!

Surgery was just the beginning.

I had more bandages, more doctor visits, and most of all, therapy that would help me learn how to use my legs and make them stronger. But I still needed more help.

That's how I met my new mom, the most important person in my life:

CONNIE!

She has a home where animals can stay while they're getting better after being sick or having surgery. It's where I met my best friends in the whole wide world.

ROLL CALL!

Molly

Montana

Montana and Molly are both learning to walk with three legs.

Toaster's back legs don't work,
but she loves to play.

Pauline is at Connie's to exercise
and learn healthy eating.

Toaster

Pauline

Meanwhile, Merv loves to chill out on the front porch.

Kerry has a silly style
all her own.

Big Moose is at Connie's for Forever Care.
He always has a huge stick in his mouth.

And it's not just dogs at Connie's!
Llamas come here to be safe from forest fires.

Izzy loves to play cowgirl with her best friend, Danny.

But my very best friend at Connie's is a three-legged Labrador named **Spree.**

Spree + Antoine = **BFF!**

Spree and I became such good friends that she went to all my doctor's appointments with me.

Even though I couldn't walk on my own, Connie took Spree and me
in the wagon to the pond every day with all the other dogs.

Someday . . .
I really wanted to be
able to go swimming.
And run.
And sniff a cat.
And roll in the grass.

Antoine

So... I kept going to therapy.

I just knew I could get through the hard parts with the help of all of my new friends.

Eventually my legs stopped hurting, and I was strong enough to get my very own wheelchair.

My legs didn't work like other dogs' but I didn't care. I could move around with my pals now!

After enough therapy, I didn't need the wheelchair anymore.
Instead, my friend, Ben, made a special brace just for me.

I've come so far, thanks to loving friends and family.
I learned to never give up!

I also learned that superheroes all have their own special powers.
Even though my legs don't work like my friends do,
we still have great fun playing together.
And that's what matters.

I play with the horses.

I dig all the holes I want in the mud.

We celebrate and even dress up for special parties.

One time Moose was crowned

FAIRY KING!

We enjoy a cake and treats made especially for dogs.

I learned that nothing can get in the way of having fun, together.

We all love car rides to pick up more treats.

Spree always gets the front seat.

I can finally go swimming!
I love to splash and chase toys with my friends.

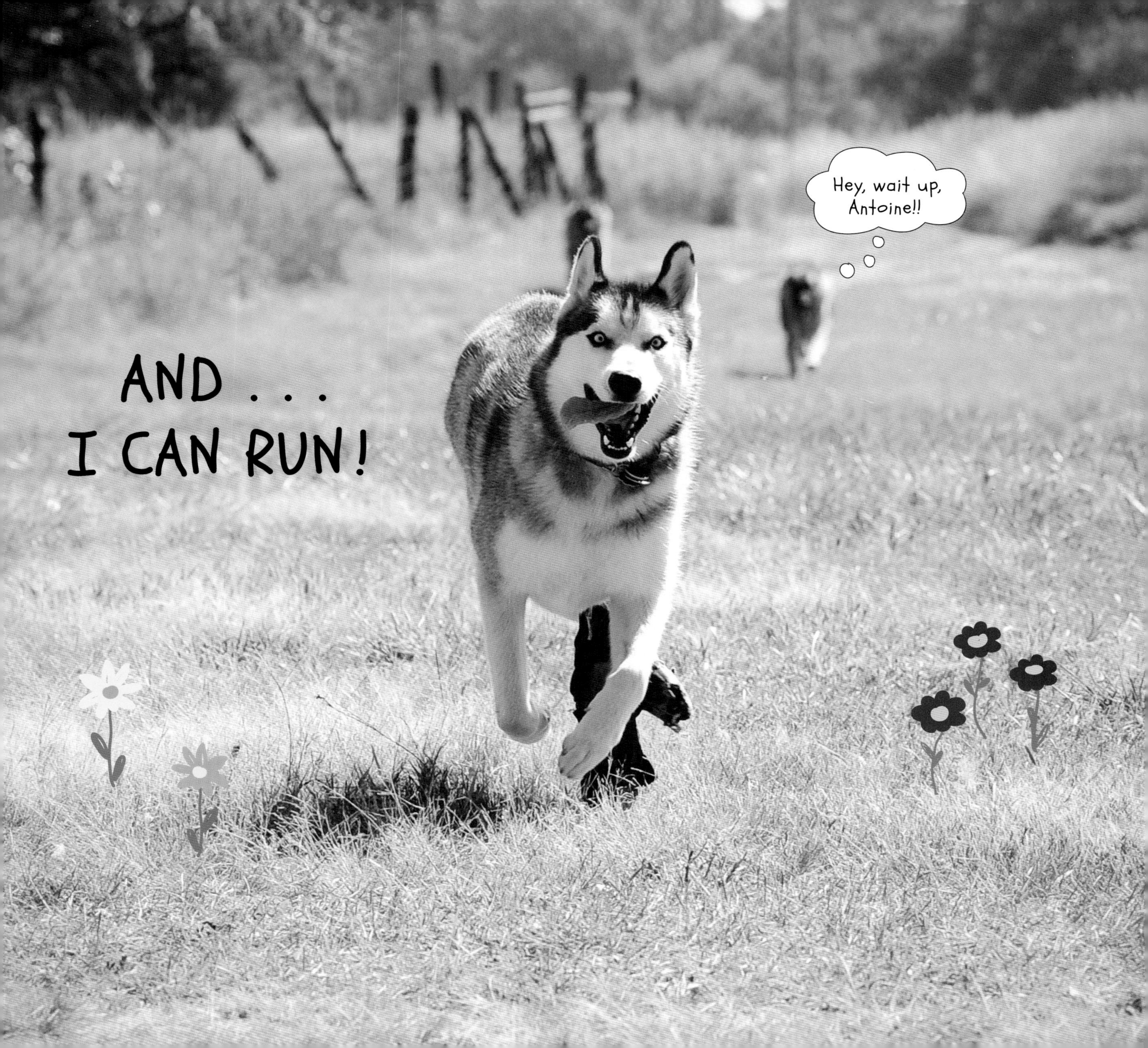
AND . . .
I CAN RUN!
Hey, wait up, Antoine!!

I roll in the grass . . .

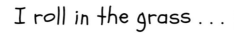

and I can even sniff a cat!

Sometimes we have to
take a bath.

UGH.

At least it's a bathtub
made just for dogs.

After a bath,
we get a massage!
Everyone loves them
and waits their turn.

And sometimes after
all our adventures,
we just need a nap.

When I'm not playing outside, I love to visit people!
I help them and teach them what I've learned.

The best part of my day
is visiting schools where
I give friendship, love,
and hugs to children
with special needs.

It's my

FAVORITE JOB!

I'm so happy that I believed in myself and worked hard.
Most of all, I learned that my differences don't stop me from being ME,

ANTOINE

THE GREAT!

Acknowledgments

I would like to thank Pat Curran for being a hero to pets and allowing all of this to happen.

Connie Fredman for providing Antoine with a house of love so he could recover and discover life.

Of course, Spree for being Antoine's forever friend.

And the following folks who have made Antoine so happy and the creation of this book seamless:

Dr. Felix Duerr, Dr. Dave Wilson—Colorado State University Veterinary Hospital

Dr. Jessica Rychel, Dr. Lindsey Fry, Erin Lines CCRP—Red Sage Integrative Veterinary Partners

Deanna Rogers, PT, CCRP, CCFT—Good Life PT for Animals

Ben Blecha—CPO Hero Braces

Elaina G Photography

Chris Schillig

Olivia Lynn

Jean Lucas and Holly Swayne

In 2003, Connie Fredman created the Canine Health Resort in Fort Collins, Colorado, to accommodate, assist, and care for pre- and postoperative patients of Colorado State University Veterinary Hospital.

Now, Connie provides care for dogs that are handicapped and receiving treatment from several veterinary facilities or those pets that are in hospice care.

She is dedicated to providing a world filled with support, daily routines, new experiences, friendships, and a cherished sense of belonging for these animals.

At the Canine Health Resort, Antoine could be a dog—not just a patient.

The author's proceeds from this book will go to Antoine's Fund—a nonprofit division of Do Good 4 Co., created to give disabled pets the opportunity to live fulfilling lives and will directly support Connie Fredman's Canine Health Resort.

For more information or to donate, follow Antoine's journey on Facebook at facebook.com/antoinestale, on Instagram at @antoinestale, or visit antoinesfund.org.